• FUN WITH
CHINESE FESTIVALS

TAN HUAY PENG

Illustrated by
LEONG KUM CHUEN

HEIAN INTERNATIONAL, INC.

© 1991 Federal Publications (S) Pte Ltd

First American Edition 1991
HEIAN INTERNATIONAL, INC.
P.O.Box 1013
Union City, CA 94587 U.S.A

ISBN 0-89346-358-2

Printed in Singapore

Well-known Singaporean cartoonist Tan Huay Peng wrote **Fun With Chinese Festivals** to show the origins, legends and stories behind the major Chinese festivals celebrated in South-east Asia. It is an informative yet light-hearted look at the quirks and myths behind such celebrations as Lunar New Year, the Dragon Boat Festival and others. Unfortunately Peng passed away in November 1990 just as he was about to complete the work. He had written on eight out of nine festivals.

So that Peng's work was not in vain, Federal Publications decided to publish the book using illustrations by another local artist, Leong Kum Chuen. Kum Chuen is an artist with *Lianhe Zaobao* and his drawings with their gentle humour complement Peng's teasingly sharp prose. To avoid disrupting Peng's distinctive, witty style , the publisher chose to exclude the last major festival, the Winter Solstice celebration, which was the one Peng had not completed.

This was Peng's last project and we dedicate this book to his memory.

Contents

Lunar New Year

Chun Jie • *Spring Festival*

The most important event in the entire Chinese festive calendar is the Lunar New Year, celebrated for fifteen days. Originally called *Chun Jie* (春节) or Spring Festival, it symbolized a time of renewed fertility of the earth — a significant event in the life of the farmer who owed his existence to the soil.

Today the Lunar New Year signifies a fresh start in life. It is a time for new hopes for a happy and prosperous new year. And to the pragmatic Chinese, what could make for greater happiness and prosperity than big money, sumptuous food and drink, and good luck?

The answer lies in remembering the saying: "To be full without overflowing is the way to keep riches."

Big Money

The shrewd Chinese mind thinks "If a little money does not go out, great money will not come in."

So people slave for money for a whole year to lavish it upon the New Year celebrations — and for good reason. With such a rousing welcome, they invoke the God of Prosperity to usher in a prosperous new year.

But for the opportunists, the truly prosperous time is the period before the celebrations. They do a roaring trade, exploiting the generous mood and raking in the profits. During this period Chinatown presents a theatrical spectacle as eager crowds throng the narrow streets, scrambling for auspicious goods and delicacies — often offered at inflated prices — in a frantic effort to lure good luck into their homes.

Pay Up

According to the Chinese, "Shame fades in the morning, but debts remain from day to day."

Nevertheless, before the old year ends all debts must be cleared to avoid shame and misfortune. New Year's Eve is one of three occasions set aside for business people to balance their books and settle accounts. (The other two special occasions are the **Dragon Boat Festival** and the **Mid-Autumn Festival**.)

In olden days, debtors who forgot to pay by the end of the year often resorted to playing hide-and-seek with their creditors; they were persistently hounded until New Year's Eve — the last chance for creditors to collect payments.

According to convention, one could no longer demand payment of a debt by New Year's Day. So desperate creditors carried lanterns even on New Year's morning to imply that it was still New Year's Eve!

Big Sweep

"**A** great fortune depends on luck; a small one on diligence" — goes the Chinese saying. The average Chinese prefers the easy way to prosperity: leave it to fortune, but never push your luck!

Good fortune favours a clean house so the family welcomes the Spring Festival with a complete spring-cleaning, a big sweep to do away with all misfortune.

All sweeping is done by New Year's Eve. To sweep on New Year's Day — an auspicious day — is to sweep away good fortune. Not only that, dust must be swept inwards from the outside, lest good luck and wealth be swept out of the house. Walls are whitewashed, doors and windows repainted. Everything must be clean or new if fortune is to smile on the family.

What a pity all the sweeping is done behind the door; if everyone swept outside his door, the city would be cleaned!

Mark Of The Fu (Luck)

Legend has it that a Ming dynasty emperor went sightseeing during the **Feast of Lanterns**. He saw, posted on a number of doors, an offensive painting of a barefooted woman with a lemon pressed to her bosom.

Feeling that the poster ridiculed the large feet of the empress, the furious emperor had the character *fu* (福) distributed only to households that did not display the poster.

An edict was then issued to massacre all families without the *fu*. From that time onward, the people deemed it a good omen to display the mark of the *fu*.

Today those who hope for an extra bit of luck display the Chinese character *fu* on the wall or the door. This character is deliberately placed upside down because *fu dao* (福倒), "luck upside down" is a pun on *fu dao* (福到), "luck arrives".

You can always rely on the fertile imagination of the Chinese to ensnare every bit of good luck!

Money In Red

No New Year celebration is complete without the traditional gift of money, wrapped up in a red packet, called *hong bao* (红包).

This is because of the proverbial power of money: "Money gives a bold front; it doesn't talk — it screams." Hence the loud red packet, symbolizing luck and prosperity — for the giver as well as the recipient.

The red packet is freely given by parents and elderly persons to their children and children of friends and relatives during the New Year calls. Married persons may give red packets to their unmarried friends.

Token sums are extended to the poor and aged as a goodwill gesture.

The amount in a red packet should be an even number to be lucky and auspicious. If the red packets are given in pairs the total amount should be an even number. Odd numbers are considered unlucky.

To reflect good upbringing, the recipient should accept the red packet graciously with the customary good wishes. It is bad manners to open red packets in the presence of the giver or other people.

It is a common practice for musicians, singers, snake-charmers and dancers to cash in on the season and perform for red packets of money.

Animal Years

In the Chinese lunar calendar, each year is named after an animal. Apparently the Buddha once summoned all living creatures to come before him but only twelve came at his bidding.

To mark their faithfulness, he named a year after each one in the order of its arrival. First came the Rat, then the Ox, Tiger, Rabbit, Dragon, Snake, Horse, Sheep, Monkey, Rooster, Dog and Boar.

The Chinese reckon ages by the lunar year so babies at birth are always one year old, whatever their birth dates. An infant born a minute before midnight on New Year's Eve is two years old on the first stroke of twelve!

Through the ages, the Chinese injected mystic meanings into the animal signs. Arbitrary interpretations were used for marriage combinations and fortune-telling.

But don't run away with the idea that the lowly Rat is less fortunate than the mighty Ox. According to a Chinese saying: "The barn rat has more grain than he can possibly eat but what does the plough ox have?"

Everybody's Birthday

If you are Chinese, you have an additional birthday: the seventh day of the new year. According to an ancient belief, the first day of the new year was the birthday of chickens; the second day, dogs; the third day, pigs; the fourth day, sheep; the fifth day, cows; the sixth day, horses; the seventh day, humans; and the eighth day, grains.

No creature was to be killed on its birthday. So no one was allowed to slaughter chicken on New Year's Day, dogs on the second day, and so on. On the seventh day — mankind's birthday — no humans were to be executed. Nothing, however, was mentioned about "killing" grains on the eighth day.

Today butchers do not slaughter pigs from New Year's Eve to New Year's Day. Most Chinese purposely reserve a surplus of cooked food on New Year's Eve for consumption on New Year's Day. (This leftover from the previous year is also a sign of abundance.)

On the seventh day — everybody's birthday — people are exhorted to eat uncooked lettuce and raw fish, especially the carp, sold at fabulous prices on this occasion. The reason: The Chinese word for fresh or raw (生) also means "life" or "grow"; therefore eating fresh vegetables and live fish is symbolic of a long and prosperous life. That is, if you have the stomach for raw fish!

Look New

The Chinese have a saying: "Give me old friends but give me new clothes."

The New Year is a time to keep old friends and discard old clothes in favour of new ones in bright auspicious colours. It is a time for a change in appearance — and personality!

New clothes therefore become a necessary feature of the celebration and everyone buys or sews new outfits, in an effort to put up a good appearance. This despite the saying: "You may change the clothes; you cannot change the man."

Abroad, the Chinese judges a man by his clothes. At home, he looks at the man's character. He doesn't worry how deceptive outward appearances can be (knowing that "good clothes open all doors").

All Things Red

New Year's Day is a red-letter day for the Chinese. To the westerner red spells danger but to the Chinese red signifies joy and luck. So red is an auspicious colour for all festive occasions.

Red banners and red lanterns herald the new year. A scarlet good-luck banner, woven with red thread and decorated with coloured tassels, is draped over the front door to ward off evil.

Red is believed to exorcise evil. It is the colour dreaded by a legendary monster which preyed on innocent victims and destroyed their properties on New Year's Eve. Hence the proverbial warning: "However bright the moon, it is better not to walk out alone, especially without a red lantern."

The New Year season is the time to adorn the house with red flowers, crimson decorations, scarlet cushion covers and fiery calligraphy scrolls. It is also a time to offer food in red containers, gifts wrapped in red paper and money in red packets, a time to flaunt a red dress and to paint, not just the house, but the whole town red.

Never mind if all these make other people see red!

Black Is Bad

Black, associated with death, is considered extremely unlucky during the New Year celebrations and should be rigorously avoided.

Don't wear or use anything black during the festive season, especially when visiting friends and relatives. (Don't worry if your hair is black.) Few people also want to turn up at funerals during this period.

The Chinese have assigned colours to the points of the compass: East is blue, West is white, North is black and South is red. (So North obviously is an unlucky direction!)

The gods are generally represented by white, goblins, red and devils', black.

Black has such bad connotations that it is often used to describe anything wicked, harmful or dirty. The Chinese believe that the hypocritical are black-hearted. They have a saying: "If you want to see black-hearted people, look among those who never miss their prayers."

But black skin is not discriminated against; the "colour of the heart" cannot be discerned by the colour of the skin.

Mind Your Tongue

Your tongue may be only six inches long but it can send a man six feet underground! As the Chinese put it: "Beneath the tongue many a man lie crushed to death." Much mischief comes from a wagging tongue.

For this reason every Chinese must exercise strict control of the tongue during the festive season; he must not only look clean, he must "sound clean". So only honeyed words are to come out of his mouth. No foul language is uttered, no unlucky words like "die" or "bad luck" spoken lest misfortune comes to the family. Scolding or cursing is definitely not allowed.

Children are warned on New Year's Eve not to quarrel, fight or speak rudely. The Chinese believe that if children are thrashed for bad behaviour on New Year's Day , then they would be inclined to be rebellious throughout the year.

However, after the festive season, the tongue may be loosened. According to the Chinese saying: "If you curse a man every day, you ensure him happiness and long life." In other words: Get the coffin ready and the man won't die!

No Sharp Ends

"**B**lessings never come in pairs; misfortunes never come singly" — laments the Chinese saying.

Therefore do not rely on your present good fortune; prepare for the year when it may leave you. And start right at the beginning of the new year in order not to "cut the thread of good fortune".

During this season, all sorts of instruments with sharp ends or edges like knives, scissors and needles are kept away. Avoid needlework if you don't want your fingers to be pricked for the rest of the year. And don't give presents with pointed or sharp ends like pens, pencils, knives or tools. All sharp instruments that may "sever" good fortune from the family are hidden away.

Take special care when handling fragile items like crockery, cups, glasses and mirrors. If anything breaks the family will break up, or seven years of bad luck or a death will occur!

If a glass is dropped on the floor and breaks, you can still turn the misfortune into a blessing if you immediately utter, like the Cantonese: "*Lok taye, hoi fa!*" meaning "Drop to the ground and burst into bloom!"

So all you who are Chinese, take heed: If you have a sharp tongue, don't use it; if you have a fragile heart, handle it with care — don't break it!

Flower Power

To the Chinese, flowers are not just botanical wonders — soft to the touch, beautiful to the eyes and fragrant to the nose. Many of them have symbolic and auspicious meaning, hence indispensable for a fortunate new year.

Flowers are offered to deities and to ancestors on New Year's Eve and left on the altars for the fifteen-day celebrations.

The most significant item is the pink "pineapple flower" called in Hokkien *ong lai hua* (凤梨花). Because it rhymes with an expression meaning "the flower that brings fortune" (旺来花), it is propitious.

Equally significant is the orchid, a symbol of love and fertility, described by Confucius as "the prince of all that are fragrant". The peony — "king of flowers" — is the symbol of spring.

Other symbolic flowers: lotus — holiness or summer; chrysanthemum — "flower of the recluse" or autumn; plum blossom — "pure and honest friend" or winter.

The Chinese still believe in good fortune through flower power even if they use artificial flowers! But they take a lesson from fresh flowers: "Man cannot be always fortunate; flowers do not last forever."

Fiery Crackers

To the Chinese, fire-crackers mean more than just glorious noise. They symbolize prosperity and good luck, besides warding off evil. Noise is a sign of life and noise-making is a work of merit.

Noise is a feature of every festivity. To herald the new year fire-crackers are set off, presumably to frighten off evil spirits but they often result in merely scaring the wits out of harmless mortals and causing pollution, fires and deaths. Even the saying warns: "Once a fire has been lit, who can order it to burn this and not burn that?"

Because of the ban on crackers in Singapore, not enough of these evil spirits are frightened off to make people happy. So the resourceful Chinese record the noise of fire-crackers on tape for harmless playback. And they add a finishing touch: a giant model of a cluster of fire-crackers in fiery red — the colour evil spirits dread!

Longevity Vigil

Long life is considered a great blessing. Longevity is often symbolized by the deer, crane, tortoise and peach. On a person's birthday noodles are eaten for long life because the long strands have an auspicious association.

The Star-god of Longevity is often pictured as issuing from a peach or as a threesome with the Star-gods of Happiness and Wealth.

On New Year's Eve, children are required to be obedient and stay awake to welcome the new year and wish their parents a happy new year after midnight. Some Chinese believe that the longer the children stay awake, the longer their parents will live. The children themselves will also live long lives.

The children do not mind keeping such a New Year vigil. The anticipation of receiving *hong baos* is enough to keep them obediently and joyfully awake. They look forward, not to a long life of years, but to a fat packet of money.

Which goes to show that everyone, even children, is obedient to money!

New Year Greetings

A universal form of Chinese New Year greeting is *Gong Xi Fa Cai* — meaning literally: "Congratulations. May your wealth increase." Belief has it that if you begin the new year well, everything you do throughout the year will be crowned with success.

Other forms of greetings are:
"Progress in the New Year."
"New Year felicitations."
"Plenty of luck in the spring."

In greeting cards the dragon, deer, bat and peaches symbolize luck, success and longevity. Besides greeting cards, the Chinese house salutes you with more good wishes which appear on silk scrolls, wooden and plastic boards and strips of red paper. Often there are decorative figurines of three beaming old men signifying happiness, success and long life, known as "The Three Stars". These are represented by single Chinese characters: *fu* (福), *lu* (禄) and *shou* (寿) — happiness, success and longevity.

The Chinese prefer New Year wishes to resolutions. If wishes were not granted they could place the responsibility on the gods; whereas when resolutions are broken they have only themselves to blame.

But as the saying goes, wishes cannot fill a sack. And if wishes were horses, then beggars would ride.

Reunion Feast

The importance of food is highlighted in the saying: "If there is no food for one day, a father's love grows cold; if there is no food for three days, a wife's love grows cold."

By the same token, if there is no reunion feast on New Year's Eve, a family's love grows cold. The reunion or *tuan nian* (团年) is therefore a demonstration of the love and respect that bind the family together. And to symbolize that unity, a big fish is usually the centrepiece against an extravagant setting of dishes.

Every member of the family makes it a duty to be present for this auspicious occasion. Even deceased ancestors are invited, and the feasting and rejoicing take place as if they were present. When all are gathered around the table, the reunion feast, usually an elaborate affair, begins amidst much talking and eating and drinking.

For once, gone are the restraints on the mouth and stomach, forgotten the proverbial warning: "Much talk brings on trouble; much food brings on indigestion."

Eating Right

Food is so important to the Chinese that it forms a part of their normal greeting: "Have you eaten yet?" To which the reply must be: "Yes, thank you" — even if it is not true.

New Year's Day begins with a meal which is usually vegetarian. To eat meat or slaughter on that day is highly inauspicious.

On New Year's Eve the food is prepared in abundance so that there will be leftovers to symbolize material wealth brought over from the previous year.

The year will get off to a bad start if you serve food in or eat from broken or chipped crockery, as this signifies your eating into your own capital. You must begin the new year well to be successful the rest of the year.

Also, the pair of chopsticks used for eating should be of the same length. Otherwise you will miss the boat — literally — whenever you should travel by sea.

So for the New Year season, don't eat to live; live to eat! Above all, remember the Chinese proverbial advice: "If you want a good meal, don't offend the cook."

Fish Of Fortune

Most Chinese live by the saying: "Money from any source smells as sweet." One source is the piquant raw fish salad prepared for the New Year called *yu sheng*.

The raw fish is thinly sliced and tossed with a mixture of shredded vegetables in a sauce of white vinegar, sugar, salt and whole peppercorns. The significance and symbolism of this exotic raw fish salad is calculated to generate money.

The Chinese word for fish, *yu* (鱼), has the same pronunciation as the word for "excess" (余). *Sheng* (生) means "life". So *yu sheng* is eaten for a long life and abundant wealth.

The dish hits the menu during the New Year season, reaching its height of popularity on the seventh day — everybody's birthday. This once-a-year dish commands an exorbitant price. To get the precious raw fish through the mouth, the consumer has to pay through the nose!

The act of tossing the raw fish is referred to as *lao qi* (捞起), "tossing up good fortune". Without doubt, *yu sheng* is the fish of fortune to the vendor because the consumer, lured by the prospects of longevity and prosperity, acts like the proverbial fish in the Chinese saying: "The fish eyes the bait, not the hook!"

Fortune Foods

A fortune is not made in a few hours but according to the Chinese, it can be made during the fifteen days of the festive season — by partaking of foods with auspicious and promising names. Here is a favoured list:

Oysters, called *ho see* (蚝) in Cantonese, can mean "fortunate occasion".

Sea-moss, or *fa cai* (发菜), sounds like the phrase meaning "to prosper".

Shiitake mushroom, or *dong gu* (冬菇), goes along with the Chinese idiom *dong cheng xi jiu* meaning "wishes fulfilled from east to west".

Red dates, or *hong zao* (红枣), can mean "prosperity comes early".

Lotus seeds, called *lian zi* (莲子), promise a family with a continuous lineage.

So does the special "New Year Greeting Fish" — desirable for its roe — which spawns prolifically during this season. It costs a small fortune in cash, but it promises a big return in offsprings.

Cake Of The Year

Nian Gao (年粿) is a circular brown cake made from rice flour and sugar. It is the cake of the New Year.

The character *gao* (糕) sounds the same as the character for "high" in Chinese; so whoever eats *nian gao* will attain a higher status or ascend to a better life in the new year.

The cake is also emblematic of complete or eternal friendship because of its round shape and glutinosity. Its stickiness suggests standing by one another through thick and thin — a mark of true friendship. Its sweetness promises the eater a sweet life.

This seasonal cake is the favourite gift for friends and relatives. The *nonyas* (Straits Chinese women) name it *kuih bakul* (basket cake in Malay). When the cake hardens after a few weeks, it can be steamed and eaten with grated coconut or cut into slices, dipped in batter and fried.

However, no matter how sticky it is, the king of cakes by any high-sounding auspicious name cannot strengthen or sweeten the bond of friendship. For as the Chinese themselves put it, "It is difficult to win a friend in a year; it is easy to offend one in an hour."

Tray Of Prosperity

During the festive season an octagonal tray is traditionally used to serve guests. The shape of the tray is significant, as eight (*paat* 八) in Cantonese sounds like "prosper" in the same dialect.

This tray contains a variety of sweetmeat, cakes and dates in each of its eight outer sectors. The central sector holds the ubiquitous melon seeds. The sweetmeat reflects the sweetness of life, the cakes or *gao* (sounds like "high") suggest a successful lifestyle, while the dates, called *zao zi* (枣子), rhyme with the phrase meaning "to have sons early" (早子).

The melon seeds, a symbol of progeny, suggest proliferation of offsprings — likened to gold and silver and a mark of prosperity. A Cantonese host invites guests to help themselves to melon seeds by saying: "Pick up silver and gold!" So the more melon seeds you eat, the more children you are likely to have.

Producing melon seeds or children, however, is one thing; bringing them up with discipline is an entirely different matter, raising the proverbial question: "From the roof-top of a house, who knows which way the melon will roll?"

The Chinese have a ready answer: "When a melon is ripe, it will drop off by itself!"

Love Letters

Love may conquer all. However, during the New Year celebrations love needs an added boost. So housewives spend precious time baking thin, crispy rice-powdered wafers fondly called "love letters" by past local Europeans and *Kuih Belanda* (Dutch cake) by the *Peranakan* (Straits Chinese).

When served, the love letters are rolled up in little scrolls or folded in fourths to look like unfolded Chinese fans. The embossed design on the circular wafer suggests the secret code between lovers.

The round shape of an unfolded love letter is significant. The Chinese character for round, *yuan* (圓) also means "satisfaction" or "a cycle of life." In Cantonese, the sound *yuan* sounds like *yuan* in *Zhuang yuan* (状元), — a minister of high rank in Imperial China. The round love letter therefore connotes success in one's cycle of life.

Baking love letters individually requires painstaking effort — truly a labour of love. So love letters are desirable mainly because, in the words of the saying, "Love values the effort, not the prize."

Oranges Of Gold

The sharing of oranges as New Year gifts is propitious if we go by the saying "A divided orange tastes just as sweet." Besides, the orange not only looks and tastes good, it has a name that sounds good.

In Cantonese, both the orange (柑) and gold (金) have the same pronunciation *gam*, which is also homonymous with "sweetness" (甘).

Oranges therefore bring sweetness and wealth if offered in pairs or even numbers.

The tangerine (橘) stands for luck because its Cantonese pronunciation *kat* sounds like "lucky" (吉). A kumquat tree in the house promises a fruitful and prosperous new year; its Cantonese name *gam kat* sounds like "golden luck". For New Year's Day, the orange has come to stay.

Health Nuts

Among the New Year delicacies is the ever-popular peanut in the pod stage. Peanuts take their name from their resemblance to peas in a pod. They also go by numerous lowly names like goober (given by African plantation slaves) and groundnuts or monkey-nuts (given by the British).

To the Americans peanuts may be just nuts, but to the Chinese they are "health nuts" and go by the flowery name *hua sheng* (花生) — the flower of life.

Metaphorically, the groundnut is elevated to *chang sheng guo* (长生果) — the nut of longevity — because of its shape, with promises of a long, healthy life.

Equating health with wealth, the Chinese saying goes: "A poor man in good health is worth at least half a rich man." But health is more a condition of mind than matter. So the picture of health requires a happy frame of mind.

Yam Seng!

Without wine inside the bottle you will not have guests inside the house, especially during the New Year season. But be warned: "Good wine ruins the purse; bad wine ruins the stomach."

The Cantonese originated the phrase "*Yam seng*" (干杯) meaning "Drink to victory or success" — often mistranslated as "Bottoms up"!

The term "bottoms up" more appropriately applies to the drunk because liquor works in two ways: it will either put you on top of the world or under the table!

The Chinese host sips tea and makes believe it is wine. To prevent trickery, a guest sometimes insists on mixing or exchanging drinks with the host, amidst much merriment.

Often the veteran drinker throws all caution to the wind, not realizing that a little liquor makes one lose inhibitions and a lot makes one give exhibitions.

Let him heed the Chinese saying: "If you want a plan to stop drinking, look at a drunken man when you are sober."

The Kitchen God

The Kitchen God is the most important of the domestic deities. He receives offerings twice a month and a special feast of honey at the end of the year, on the twenty-third or twenty-fourth day of the twelfth moon. He is represented by a portrait or a slip of red paper with the necessary characters.

As the old year draws to a close, the Kitchen God appears before the heavenly Jade Emperor to present his annual report on the behaviour of members of a household.

To get into his good books, worshippers clean his shrine in the kitchen thoroughly. They sweeten his mouth with honey to ensure that his words will be sweet and flattering.

If they fear a bad report, they try to muzzle his mouth by wiping it with honey or sticky confection, or get him drunk by dipping his portrait in wine — or both.

Some go a step further: they burn a generous amount of spirit money to help him with travelling expenses. Sometimes a paper horse is thrown in for good measure — for the celestial agent to ride on in comfort.

The Chinese practise what they preach: "With money you can make spirits turn the mill." To them, much money — even spirit money — moves the gods!

The Money God

The God of Wealth, the most widely worshipped deity among the Chinese, ranks highest in the celestial ministry of finance.

He was reputed to have been a warrior, riding a black tiger and hurling pearls that exploded like bombs. Notwithstanding his powers, he was killed by an opposing general and his status was raised to celestial president of the ministry of riches.

Associated with this much-adored deity is the money tree, with branches of coins strung together and fruits of gold ingots, all ready to be shaken down.

His birthday is on the fifth day of the New Year and elaborate feasts are prepared in his honour on the fourth day. One curious custom is the hanging of live fish over the offering. The fish are then returned to spawn and proliferate. The fish symbolize abundance because "fish" and "abundance" have the same pronunciation *yu*.

Farmers and villagers believe the God of Wealth controls the wealth of the world, distributing it to each family once a year. It is the hope of getting a larger portion during the coming year that each family worships him so devoutly. And the New Year is the opportune time to honour him with the best that money can buy. As the saying goes: "With money you can influence the gods; without it you cannot summon a man."

The Triple Rites

Of all the New Year rituals, the most important are the triple rites: the offerings to the ancestors, to earth and heaven, and to the God of Wealth.

The offering to the ancestors — a gesture of remembrance, respect and gratitude — is also a request for continued protection. Favourite dishes are placed before the ancestral tablets, and joss sticks, candles and spirit money are burnt.

The offering to earth and heaven ensures favourable weather and a bumper harvest. On the altar are placed bowls of rice with chopsticks, cups of tea and wine, dried fruit and fresh oranges.

Besides the joss sticks, incense burner and spirit money, also included is the latest edition of the Chinese Almanac.

In expectation of a greater share of riches, worshippers invite the God of Wealth home on the fourth day of the New Year to partake of the sumptuous feast offered in his honour.

Generous offerings of food and spirit money are also made to the five evil gods of plague to placate them. Whatever the cost, they must be dissuaded from causing misfortune and sickness in the new year.

And here is the secret of handling evil spirits the Chinese way: "Give the devil enough money, and he'll push the mill-stone."

Family Ties

An old Chinese saying raises the problem of running a family: "It is easier to govern a nation than to rule a family." New Year visits are an attempt to reinforce family ties.

The first day is for the family only and is devoted to feasting and visiting relatives. The ancestors also are honoured with new red scrolls inscribed with long-life and prosperity signs. Door-god posters are stuck outside the front door to ward off evil spirits.

Family members amuse themselves playing music, cards and mahjong. While children receive red packets of money, adults snack on New Year sweets and delicacies.

The second day is also for the family and usually features a banquet-style family feast, but friends and acquaintances may visit and exchange good wishes.

The third day is considered one in which family members might quarrel — a reasonable supposition after two days of continuous and monotonous togetherness. So everyone goes out to visit and wish friends prosperity.

But remember the ancient Chinese secret of prosperity: "Only he who knows the meaning of enough is truly prosperous."

Happiness & Prosperity

The pursuit of happiness through prosperity seems to be the obsession of the Chinese during the New Year season.

On the fourth day many shops open for business. The more enterprising ones choose to open on the second day – even if only for a short time — so that they can carry on business on the odd third day without being unlucky.

The fifth day is also considered the birthday of the Money God. People heartily receive and welcome him with offerings of incense, sacrifices and spirit money — with hopes of a prosperous new year.

The seventh day is designated "Everybody's Birthday". This calls for another family meal of raw fish — with hopes for prosperity and long life.

The New Year festivities culminate with the *Yuan Xiao* (元宵), the first full moon of the New Year, on the 15th Night (*Chap Goh Meh*). *Yuan Xiao* is also known as the Lantern Festival.

The emphasis of the New Year celebrations on money seems to imply that money brings happiness. Many choose to ignore the Chinese proverbial advice: "So long as there is bread to eat, water to drink and an arm to sleep on, happiness is not impossible."

Lantern Festival

Yuan Xiao • *Lantern Festival*

The New Year celebrations wind up in a grand finale on the first full moon of the year called *yuan xiao* (元宵), also known as the Lantern Festival. Locally it is *Chap Goh Meh* — Hokkien for "fifteenth night". *Chap Goh Meh* used to be celebrated with pomp and a showy display.

Houses were brilliantly lit and lanterns hung over the five-foot-ways; feasts and parties were thrown on a lavish scale. Everyone, young and old, looked forward to going out on this entrancing moonlight night.

The evening was heralded by the unrestrained firing of crackers to exorcise lurking monsters and evil spirits. The highlight was the parade of young, single people, as girls were allowed to go out and socialize — chaperoned, of course.

Under the influence of the bewitching full moon, love at first sight filled the air. Professional matchmakers soon got down to business, armed with the blessings of parents insistent on enforcing the saying: "A maiden marries to please her parents; a widow to please herself."

Feast Of Lanterns

The Lantern Festival probably originated when Emperor Ming Huang of the Tang dynasty built thirty staggering lantern towers to celebrate the new year's first full moon. The lanterns took the forms of dragons, phoenixes, tigers and leopards, dangling and prancing in the air. On another occasion, a lantern wheel sixty metres high was erected with 50,000 hanging lanterns! Over 2,000 young girls sang under the lantern wheel for three days and nights.

In certain provinces, families lit up as many lanterns as there were family members. And if they desired more children, they would hang extra lanterns. The lanterns displayed varied in sizes and designs. Many were extremely mobile, ingeniously designed and cleverly crafted — a tribute to human's fertile imagination.

But no matter how showy or imposing, the lantern is just a paper lantern. So if you tend to emulate the showy lantern, heed the proverbial warning: "Do not thrust your finger through your own paper lantern!"

Night Of Freedom

The Lantern Festival, an indispensable feature of *Yuan Xiao*, originated as a ceremony to usher in the increasing light and warmth of the season after the winter's cold. It was part of festivities honouring the Sun God.

But political upheavals during the Han dynasty at one festival made the day even more auspicious. Emperor Wen was enthroned on the fateful day and curfew was imposed at night to protect him from foul play.

To commemorate his enthronement each year, the emperor would lift the nightly curfew and mingle with the people in the streets incognito. While the people called this night *Fang Ye* (放夜) or "Night of Freedom", the emperor preferred to name it *Yuan Xiao* — "the first full moon".

Ascribing glory and freedom to the first full moon, the ancient Chinese saying goes: "The light of a hundred stars does not equal the light of the moon."

"The Night of Freedom" liberated man from the worship of the sun, only to lead him into bondage to the moon!

Romantic Wishes

When the first full moon of the year beams radiantly upon earthlings, it is the opportune time for young lovers to make their heartfelt wishes come true. The God of Destiny rises to heaven about this time to fulfil hearts' desires and the Goddess of the Sea is ready to grant wishes.

If a young woman wished for a compatible husband, she would cast oranges into the sea or river and utter the magic couplet:

"Good oranges I throw;
Good spouse will follow."

Similarly, young men would throw apples in return for a "good" wife.

For the good things in life, one would throw longans ("dragon eyes") and make the wish:

"Dragon's eyes I throw;
A good life to follow."

Dragons are highly auspicious symbols to the Chinese. Couples could also cast red dates, saying:

"These dates we cast away;
All good things come our way."

For a house one would throw pebbles and repeat the formula:

"These stones I throw;
Bungalows galore."

And for good measure, why not throw in the following wish:

"These few coins I cast away;
Much money come my way."

Moon-Made Marriages

Marriages are made in heaven, some say. Exactly where in heaven only the Chinese can tell you: It's right on the moon. And the venerable Old Man on the Moon is the Registrar of Marriages. This Old Man has everybody's record in safe keeping; he can tell who will marry whom.

By night the Old Man ties a magical and invisible red thread around the legs of newborn girls and boys. When they grow up they will be drawn together by a powerful bond: should their paths cross, a wedding is the inevitable outcome. Even if they come from embittered families or different countries, their marriage will be permanent and happy.

Beware the magic of the first full moon; the Old Man's spell joins moonstruck couples according to his register. Traditionally this was the night for young hearts to meet. Leave the rest to the Old Man on the Moon!

Sweet, Sticky Symbol

Tang Yuan (汤圆) is a syrupy dish of glutinous rice-flour balls with different sweet fillings. Served on various occasions, including *Yuan Xiao*, it has a folk-tale to add spice to it.

A palace maid named Yuan Xiao once attempted to take her own life because she missed her family. Dong Fang, a courtier, thought of a plan to help her. Following instructions, Yuan Xiao disguised herself in a red dress as the God of Fire who was ordered by the heavenly Jade Emperor to burn down the city on the sixteenth day of the New Year.

Advised by Dong Fang, the emperor decreed that every household prepare and sacrifice *tang yuan* to appease the God of Fire. And to hoodwink the heavenly Jade Emperor, all were to hang lanterns outdoors and display fireworks to give the illusion of the city burning.

Everything went according to plan. And when Yuan Xiao's family turned up for the celebration they were all reunited.

That is another reason why the fifteenth day celebration is known as *Yuan Xiao* and *tang yuan* came to be a symbol of family reunion and affection.

So when you next eat *tang yuan*, remember: you are partaking of the fare of gods, the favourite delicacy of the God of Fire. And in the eyes of the Jade Emperor, when you light lanterns or fireworks, you are setting your house on fire!

Living By Lantern Light

Two customs associated with the Lantern Festival provide food for thought and for the stomach.

The first is an old literary game called "Guessing the Lantern's Riddle" or *Cai Deng Mi* (猜灯谜). Riddles were written on slips of paper and pasted lightly onto lanterns with clues and hints. The riddles were based on the Chinese language, historical personalities and places. Anyone who guessed correctly was rewarded right on the spot.

The second is an old custom called "Eating Yam under the Lanterns". Around midnight, family members would gather under the brightest lantern to eat soft-boiled yams. This apparently prevented the soul's transmigration which, Buddhists believe, follows one's death.

Lanterns were signposts for guests and spirits of ancestors, to guide them to the lunar celebrations. After a sumptuous fifteen-day feast the spirits were guided back by lantern light to the world beyond.

Many Chinese practise ancestor worship and offer food sacrifices to the dead. If only they would recall their own proverbial utterance: "The living man doesn't know his soul; the dead man doesn't know his corpse."

Chingay Parade

The Chinese have a saying: "Pleasure is shallow, trouble deep." Despite that, the Chinese have a way of drowning deep trouble in shallow pleasure.

And pleasure during the Lantern Festival does not only mean eating with the mouth, it also means feasting with the eyes. The spectacular *Chingay* — meaning "decorations" — parade is a sight for sore eyes.

The Chingay celebrates with stilt walkers, flower girls, agile acrobats, lively lion and dragon dances, and dozens of decorated floats taking to the streets in colourful pageantry,

accompanied by clashing cymbals, gongs and drums. Heading the exotic procession is a huge triangular flag on a giant bamboo pole, skilfully supported and balanced by a stalwart bearer.

But it is the male stilt dancers that steal the show — some with false beards and painted faces and others masquerading as women, all cavorting about with an amusing gait. They infect the audience with the carnival spirit.

Lion Dance

The Lion Dance associated with the Feast of Lanterns is most loved by the Chinese. The lion is a symbol of a bodhisattva (an ascetic) and acts as a guardian of Buddhism. The Lion Dance is also called "Game of the Lion" which, in its earliest form, was a demon-expelling ritual.

In a lion dance, two dancers form the body of an ornate cloth lion and another postures in front with a huge, decorated ball representing the sun or a priceless pearl. To the heavy beat of gongs and drums the lion prances in pursuit of the pearl, displaying remarkable acrobatics, with eyeballs rolling, tongue flapping, jaws clacking and bells tinkling.

Today the Lion Dance has lost much of its religious significance and it is not difficult to see through the little "game of the lion". As the lion prances along the street, it "threatens" shops and stalls along its route. And the only way to "pacify" the voracious lion is to shove red packets of money down its throat.

Instead of chasing off evil spirits, the lion seems bent on chasing after material wealth, symbolized by the pearl, a far cry from the sobering Chinese precept: "Even he who has accumulated ten thousand taels of silver cannot take with him at death half a copper cash."

All Souls' Day

Qing Ming • *All Souls' Day*

Q*ing Ming* (清明) — literally "pure brightness" — is also known as All Souls' Day.

Originally it was a celebration of spring, falling in early April, 106 days after the winter solstice. It is more a picnic than a festival — a happy day in the open as families go to their ancestors' cemeteries and tidy the graves, place red candles and joss-sticks on the stone altar and offer food, drinks and flowers. This is to remember and "help" the deceased in their "other" world. But first the Soil God has to be appeased with an offering so that he won't take the food reserved for the ancestors.

In olden days flageolet-players, ready to pipe a dirge for a fee, joined the festivities at the cemeteries. Occasionally professional wailers would put up their mourners-by-proxy act. Families also burn joss-paper to "deposit money" in their ancestors' "hell banks" so that grandpa — an incorrigible spendthrift on earth — will have some spare change in the other world.

While waiting for the ancestors to feast on the food, family members picnic at the gravesite. Then they pack back all the food for another feast. The Chinese are a practical and sensible people. They believe in making everybody, including themselves, happy. And when it comes to food, they subscribe to the saying: "Waste not, want not."

Gravesite "Wind and Water"

"**T**he prosperity of a man's descendants depends on the position of his house and the position of his grave" — goes the old Chinese saying.

The Chinese consider the dead as living and the grave as their abode. They will not build a house or site a grave without first consulting a geomancer — a fortune-teller who reads the forces of "wind and water" or *feng shui* (风水) on the occupant of any space. To disrupt the forces of nature by building on the earth or digging into it would run the risk of being affected by "bad wind and water". It takes an "expert" to pick an auspicious site for the grave and the day to start excavating.

Consider how "wind and water" affect the lifestyle of a Chinese businessman:

His working place could be a small, shabby office auspiciously sited in Chinatown to churn out money. His living place is likely to be a magnificent mansion with a protruding tortoise-head to ensure longevity. And his resting place: a huge, ornate grave, well-sited to offset the long-term and wide range effects of bad *feng shui*.

To rest in peace, he must have a grave on a south-facing hillside with protective walls on each side to keep off east and west winds. It should also be located over an underground water source.

To be sure, *feng shui* is not just "wind and water"; it means money — tossed by wind, drained by water! To further show their skepticism, the down-to-earth Chinese have this last word: "The fortune-teller dies in the prime of life; the *feng shui* man has no grave."

Gravesite Spring-Cleaning

The Chinese have a definition for life and death: "Living is a spring dream; dying is like going home."

The resting place or "home" needs a spring-cleaning once a year and every family member has a hand in this. So on Qing Ming Day entire families, hoes and other tools in hand, start out early in the morning to tidy up the area around their ancestors' tombs. They uproot weeds, wipe the tomb stone and site, and offer food and flowers. Yellow ribbons believed to stave off homeless, wandering spirits neglected by their own descendants are placed on the end of a bamboo stick, or kept in place by a stone, on top of the tomb. Homeless spirits can behave like mischievous hooligans and vandals.

Cremation used to be practised only by Buddhist monks or as a punishment for criminals. Today land is getting scarce not only for the living but also for the dead.

The time has come when people can no longer echo the Chinese saying: "Any place in the yellow earth will do to bury a man." Eventually columbarium or temple visits will replace cementary visits. No more yellow earth for the dead; no more gravesite spring-cleaning.

Ancestor Worship

Confucius emphasized paying homage to ancestors. Expounding his concept of *li* (礼) or propriety, he taught: "Filial piety means obedience; in serving one's parents while alive according to propriety, in burying them when dead according to propriety, and in sacrificing to them according to propriety." The living were further asked to "serve the dead as they were served when alive".

Following this code, Qing Ming becomes an occasion for the worship of ancestors. The dead are worshipped and offered food and wine which are in turn consumed by the offerers. On other occasions, these offerings are placed before ancestral tablets in the home's family altar. Ancestral tablets are usually small wooden boards inscribed with birth and death dates. This altar will include the ancestors' names and photographs.

The Chinese are obsessed with the dead. To them, the living and the dead are bound by mutual dependence; a smooth and happy relationship with the dead is important. Although ancestor worship is described as respect for the dead, it indicates a fear of the dead — a fear that the dead, if not placated, will return to harm the living. Filial piety may well be involved but the bottom line is still fear.

While the matter-of-fact Chinese will exhort you to worship your ancestors, in the same breath they will quote the Chinese saying: "If you do not support your parents while alive, it is no use sacrificing to them when dead."

Hell Money

Hell money paves the way for the dead in their dealings with other spirits. How its use came about dates to the legend that an old man from the "other world" helped child prodigy Wang Bo (王勃) excel in a literary competition. In return he asked the boy for monetary help to settle a gambling debt of $10,000 with the Chang Lu Spirit (长芦神). On his way out the boy forgot his promise. A flock of crows promptly blocked his way. Wang Bo then remembered the old man's request and immediately burnt mock money or joss paper at the Chang Lu Temple.

Joss paper, imprinted with silver, is usually folded into silver-ingot shapes to facilitate burning. Traditionally, it is made of cheap paper with a patch of gold overprint with a red pattern.

Today, "spirit money" is available as banknotes on good paper. These banknotes are in Chinese and English. Issued by the "Ming Tong Bank (冥通银行) in hell", they incorporate the following information: "Currency for the Other World: HELL BANK NOTE." Large-sized hell banknotes, printed in full-colour and including pictures of "hell banks" and portraits of Confucius, are also issued in denominations of thousands of million.

Whether or not spirit money will give way to cheques and credit cards in a cashless spirit society, only the dead can tell. One thing, though, the Chinese are sure of: "Money will open a blind man's eyes and make a priest sell his prayer books. Money can corrupt the spirits."

Paper Treasures

Up till the end of the Sui period (AD 617), genuine articles were burnt for the dead. Fortunately a message apparently came from the other world that: "Paper impressed with yellow tin foil is a good substitute for genuine silk fabric. Men and spirits are not the same. For the spirits, counterfeits are preferable to genuine articles."

Since then, the offerings have become symbolically most opulent. Not only paper houses are burnt for the spirit world but also temples. (This occurred in a ceremony in Ang Mo Kio, Singapore, during the inauguration of a new clan temple. The ancestral spirits needed a temple in the "other world" to assist their earthbound relatives!)

It is not uncommon today to despatch glittering mansions (made with shiny paper) through fire, followed by a retinue of servants to make life easier for the deceased. Before consigning these paper servants to the flame, each effigy is given a name while its ear is pricked. Other gifts sent by fire include televisions, hi-fi systems, video and tape recorders, computers and calculators, refrigerators — anything to make life in the other world pleasurable. If an airplane is included, with it goes its pilot. And, of course, a limousine would not be complete without a chauffeur.

Cold Food Feast

The Cold Food Feast (寒食节) occurs on the eve of Qing Ming. On this day the story of its origin is recounted. It is the tragic story of Jie Zi Dui (介子推), a loyalist who lived in Shanxi Province in 600 BC. Jie saved his starving lord's life by a noble act of sacrifice. When his lord became the ruler of a small principality, he decided to honour and reward Jie. Jie declined, preferring to lead a hermit's life with his mother.

A search party was sent after him but Jia fled, bearing his mother on his back and hiding in the forest of Mount Mian. A fire was started in an attempt to smoke them out. When the fire had burnt itself out after three days and nights, mother and son were found as they had died — with their arms thrown round a willow tree. To honour Jie posthumously, the grief-stricken lord erected a spiritual tablet — the forerunner of ancestral tablets.

On the anniversary of Jie's death, all fires in homes were ordered to be put out. As there were no fires, the people had to eat uncooked food — "cold food". But to warm their hearts, the story of Jie was passionately retold.

The loyalty of this humble man who preferred death to capitulation is often cited to reinforce the saying: "The loyal minister fears not death; he who does fear death is not a loyal minister."

Willow Power

Ever since Jie Zie Dui died embracing a willow tree, the willow is believed to have miraculous power over demons and can expel them as occasion demands.

During Qing Ming bunches of willow branches are often used to sweep the tombs. Willow twigs or leaves are hung on front doors to ensure clear sight for the house's occupants. Farmers did it to forecast rain or drought.

Families going out wear a bouquet of willow twigs or leaves. If you fail to wear willow in some shape or form on Qing Ming Day, you will be reborn as a yellow dog, it is believed.

In ancient China, it was the custom to offer someone going away a sprig of willow leaves. To cure lunacy, believed to be caused by malicious spirits, patients were thrashed with willow leaves or twigs.

However, the Chinese themselves have a surer but more difficult way: "If you shout loudly three times 'I don't want money', even the devil will fear you!"

Qing Ming Kite-Flying

Every Chinese festival is an occasion for rejoicing — even one connected with death. Thus Qing Ming is a time for many more activities than just morbid grave-sweeping. In olden days these included ball games, cock-fighting, dog-racing, swings and especially kite-flying.

When kites were first made in China, Li Ye adapted a whistle for the kite to produce a sound like that of the *zheng*, a zither-like instrument. There lies the origin of the modern name for the kite: *feng zheng* (风筝) or "wind zither".

Kites come in a variety of shapes and sizes: butterflies, frogs, centipedes, fishes and even historical and legendary figures. The kite may be ten metres long and operated by separate lines.

The kite becomes a scapegoat, symbolically loaded with malignant forces. When it is flown high up and the string cut, it carries away its load of evil. With such an expedient way to get rid of evil, the Chinese need never worry.

Besides that, Qing Ming, as its name suggests, is a "clear and bright" day for kite-flying — a time to be uplifted, if we go by the ambitious Chinese saying: "If the string is long, the kite flies high."

Dragon Boat Festival

Duan Wu Jie • *Dragon Boat Festival*

The Dragon Boat Festival or *Duan Wu Jie* (端午节) falls on the fifth day of the fifth lunar month. Its origin dates to the legendary death of a poet-patriot around 278 B.C. Qu Yuan (屈原), an honest minister, was undermined in his efforts to fight corruption in the state of Chu. Slandered by false accusations, he was disgraced and banished.

In his twenty years of exile, the heartbroken Qu Yuan helplessly observed the state systematically destroyed from within. In despair he drowned himself in the Mi Luo River, but not before writing some of the finest poetry in Chinese literature.

Hundreds of "dragon boats" searched for his body. The people beat gongs to frighten the "River Dragon" into returning Qu Yuan. They threw overboard rice dumplings wrapped in leaves to divert the fish from eating the patriot.

Today the Chinese hold dragon boat races to commemorate the event. But more importantly, they remember Qu Yuan by eating dumplings filled with meat, eggs, chestnuts, beans and spices on Dragon Boat Day.

Originally the fifth lunar month was the time for an "Early Rain" Festival to please the River Dragon. So what started as a festival to the River Dragon now commemorates the tragic end of a patriot who, in his lifetime, was trodden on like a snake. To quote the Chinese saying: "What begins with a dragon's head often ends with a snake's tail."

Fine $500

Fine $500

Patriotic Poet

During China's Period of the Warring States, the states of Chu and Qin fought. Despite Qu Yuan's warnings, the Prince of Chu accepted Qin's invitation to ceasefire negotiations which turned out to be a trap. The unwary Prince was captured and died in captivity.

Witnessing the corruption of Chu's imperial administration, Qu Yuan expressed his rage and melancholy through poetry. In the spring of 278 B.C., when the armies of Qin occupied the capital of Chu, all hope was lost. Smitten with grief, Qu Yuan wrote two famous odes: *Ai Ying* (哀郢) and *Huai Sha* (怀沙), lamenting the fall of Ying and disclosing his suicide plan.

With a heavy heart, he proceeded to the Mi Luo River to end his life. A fisherman who met him asked: "Are you not a minister? Why should you seek a watery grave?" Qu Yuan replied: "The whole country is corrupt, except me. The people are inebriated, except me. So it's better this way." "In that case, why not move with the trend and rise in power?" But Qu Yuan preferred to sink in the river. He clasped a huge stone and jumped into the waters.

This incident happened on the fifth day of the fifth moon, marking the tragic end of a state and its loyal minister. If only the Prince of Chu had listened to the saying: "It is the minister who must reprove the prince, not the prince his minister!"

Rice Dumplings

Of all the customs associated with the Dragon Boat Festival, the most widespread is the making and eating of *zong zi* (粽子) — glutinous rice dumplings wrapped in bamboo leaves in a pyramid shape.

The origin of *zong zi* relates to Qu Yuan's death. Legend has it that about 40 B.C. a man who called himself a minister appeared before fishermen. He revealed that, although it was proper to pay homage to Qu Yuan, the rice offering invariably was eaten by the River Dragon. The proper way was to insert the rice into bamboo stems, closing the opening with chinaberry leaves tied with five-coloured threads the dragon monster dreads.

For human consumption palm leaves were used to wrap the rice into pyramid-shaped dumplings. These were called *zong zi* because *zong* is a homonym of the character for palm (棕). In time these dumplings came to be wrapped in bamboo leaves.

Today varieties of dumplings include a savoury one of glutinous rice with meat and beans; the bean variety; and the lye variety, the smallest, is yellowish-green and made of glutinous rice preserved in an alkaline solution.

Savoury dumplings have wormed their way to the Chinese heart through the stomach. Today they are consumed throughout the year by the hungry who have never even heard of Qu Yuan. The Chinese proverb suggests: "Hunger is cured by food, ignorance by study." To this the hungry Japanese add their tribute: "Dumplings are preferred to beautiful apple blossoms."

River Dragon

The ancient Chinese had a saying: "One dragon may hold back a thousand rivers."

They believed a dragon controlled the rivers and the rains. Sacrifices were offered to the River Dragon on the Summer Solstice preceding the rainy season, as farmers hoped to be favoured by timely rainfall with neither drought nor flood. Thus the River Dragon came to be adopted as deity and totem.

The Chinese concept of the dragon is rooted in its early function as a totem of a clan or tribe. Other animals worshipped were the snake, horse, deer, dog, fish and bird.

As the tribes combined under the snake tribe, their totems also underwent a metamorphosis. Although wormlike in appearance, the Chinese dragon had the body of a snake; the head, mane and tail of a horse; the horns of a deer; the paws of a dog; and scales of a fish. And it could fly like a bird!

Eventually the dragon became the emblem of imperial power. The emperors were referred to as "dragon-faced" men who sat on the "dragon throne" and ascended to heaven on "the back of a dragon". Because of such overwhelming association with power, the dragon came to symbolize success, wealth and importance.

Now you know why the Chinese often utter the proverbial saying: "With money you are a dragon; without it you are a worm."

Dragon Boat Race

Without the Dragon Boat Race there would be no Dragon Boat Festival. Dragon boats are long, narrow boats shaped and painted like dragons. They may be up to thirty metres long and can seat eight to fifteen pairs of oarsmen. The craft is paddled to the accompaniment of drums and gongs.

After the deadly plague, the Chinese believed that dragon boat races held during the festival would amuse the River Dragon and protect them from the scourge.

Fishermen used to shave their heads and tattoo their bodies to pose as dragons, hoping that dragons would mistake them for their kind and not harm them. Each year sacrificial rites were initiated to propitiate the Dragon God.

Fear is a recurrent theme in Chinese dealings with powerful dragons and dragon-like emperors. Like dragons, tyrannical rulers have to be appeased to prevent their plaguing their shrimp-like subjects. Powerful though they may be, such rulers do get into trouble, prompting the saying: "When the dragon is stranded in shallow waters, the shrimps have the last laugh."

Evil Month

"When fortune is good, you rule over the devils," goes the old saying. "When fortune is bad, they rule over you."

In China the fifth month was designated the Evil Month (恶月) when evil spirits ruled over unfortunate humans. It was the time of hot, steamy weather, conducive to the spread of infectious diseases brought — it was believed — by the Five Gods of Plague.

To counteract these five evil gods, the Chinese adopted a cunning five-pronged strategy:

(1)   Realgar, a reddish mineral, was burnt; its yellow smoke and obnoxious odour were enough to drive away demons — and exterminate insects;

(2)   Portraits of Zhong Kui, the demon-slayer, or yellow strips of paper inscribed with incantations to exorcise demons, were posted inside and outside the house;

(3)   Using the image of evil to combat evil, cakes in the likeness of the "five poisonous creatures" were eaten: the scorpion, snake, centipede, lizard and toad (or spider);

(4) Mugwort leaves, calamus and garlic placed over the door acted as antidotes to poisonous influences;

(5) A bouquet of four kinds of green leaves plus one posy of flowers (making five) hung over the doorway helped to expel demons.

The fifth day of the fifth month is considered an unlucky birthday for children. And the result of invoking spirit power against spirits? In the words of the Chinese saying: "The children of cunning sorcerers are killed by evil spirits; the children of able doctors die of ordinary diseases."

Seven Sisters Festival

Qi Qiao Jie • *Seven Sisters Festival*

The Festival of the Seven Sisters or *Qi Qiao Jie* (乞巧节) is based on the legend of the Cowherd (牛郎) and the Weaving Maiden (织女).

The Weaving Maiden was the youngest and most beautiful of the seven daughters of the Sun God. She married the Cowherd and so devoted to each other were the couple that they neglected their daily duties. They were banished to stars separated by the Milky Way.

This romantic festival, celebrated on the seventh night of the seventh month, commemorates the annual reunion of the lovers.

On this night singles pray for good spouses and happy marriages. Chinese maidens pray that the night be clear with no rain. But if it does rain, they rationalize that the couple have already come together and the rain represents their parting tears.

The Chinese do not try to explain how the Weaving Maiden, who is dependent on the supplications of humans, can ever bring love and romance into the life of humans. They are too touched by this love story that inspires a romantic festival and they see it through the eyes of the lovelorn. As they themselves express in the proverb: "The lover sees only beauty in the beloved."

The Cowhered And The Weaving Maid

This legend, with its many variations, was born out of star-gazing by the ancient Chinese. Its description of the tragic love affair between two stars, Altair and Vega, developed into a full-fledged romance. Altair and Vega are the brightest stars in the constellations Aquilla and Lyra of the Milky Way.

The Weaving Maid (Vega), seventh daughter of the Sun God, was a beautiful as she was bright. She passed her days weaving brocades with the colourful clouds in the skies. One day she peeped down upon the earth, saw the handsome Cowherd (Altair), and straightaway took a fancy to him. It was love at first sight.

Her august father allowed them to marry. But the couple were so enamoured of each other that they neglected their work and duty, spending most of their time daydreaming.

The great god separated the pair, sentencing them to live apart thereafter with the Silver Streams (Milky Way) between them. But they were allowed to see each other once a year — on the seventh night of the seventh month.

On this night, if the skies were clear the birds of heaven formed a bridge over the streams to unite the lovers. If it rained, the Silver Stream would rise and become so wide that the bridge could not be formed. Then the couple had to wait for another year. But their love remained immortally young and eternally patient.

Certainly a beautiful fairy tale — the result of much imaginative star-gazing!

Maidens' Prayer

"**A**t seventeen or eighteen, there are no ugly maidens" — declares the Chinese saying. Notwithstanding that, young maidens still pray for beauty and love. And their hearts' desire can be fulfilled on the seventh night of the seventh month by the Weaving Maid who had experienced true love.

Qi Qiao Jie has special significance for single girls, providing an opportunity to pray for good husbands and happy marriages. In days gone by the seventh night was an occasion when girls placed their best examples of weaving and sewing before the family altar, loading the altar-table with seven plates of vegetables, fruit, sweets and a mixture of beauty aids and sewing tools.

There were also group celebrations by members of so-called Seven Sisters Associations, comprising single girls, who put up colourful "shrines" to honour the celestial lovers.

A unique practice among Cantonese virgins was to communicate with the Seven Sisters through prayer and incantations. A number of theses maidens, ideally seven, would sit around a table with an altar. Offerings included seven kinds each of: flowers, bean-sprout dishes, plates of rice-shoots, cups of tea, coloured hair-braiding threads and types of cosmetics.

In a trance induced by a medium, they were supposed to descend to purgatory, ascend to heaven to obtain blessings from the Seven Sisters, and then return to earth — within a few minutes!

The explanation probably lies in the words of the Chinese proverb: "Heaven and purgatory are all within the heart."

Seven Sisters Magic

Beauty aids that can make single girls irresistibly attractive and holy water that has magical properties — these are some miracles for which devotees of the Seven Sisters pray.

Associations made up of single girls used to get together annually to commemorate the reunion of the Cowherd and the Weaving Maid. Devotees took pains to produce miniatures in sets of seven for the sisters: seven suits of garments and seven identical sets of paper paraphernalia representing powder, rouge, mirror, comb, shoes, bracelet and necklace.

On an altar-table would be a miniature bridge for the celestial lovers to cross and unite, also bowls of fruits, flowers and cakes. A pot of bean-sprouts and rice-shoots ensured prosperity and good harvests. Also on display were real perfumes, lipsticks, rouge and powder — ready to be blessed by the Seven Sisters. These would make the lucky users instantly and doubly attractive to their loved ones.

A conspicuous item was a bottle of water called the "Seven Sisters Water"; if blessed by the Sisters the water would have curative power. Such "holy water" initially should be drawn from a well after the cock's first crow.

But single girls today would have more use for the beauty aids than the "holy water". However, in seeking beauty as an aid to husband-hunting, they have missed the point of the Chinese proverb: "Beauty does not ensnare men; men ensnare themselves."

Hungry Ghosts Festival

Zhong Yuan Jie • *Mid-Year Festival*

The Mid-Year Festival or *Zhong Yuan Jie* (中元节) falls on the seventh month of the Chinese Almanac. It is better known as the Hungry Ghosts Festival.

The main rituals of this major occult festival are held on the 15th and the festival lasts a whole month. During this period the gates of hell or purgatory are believed to be opened and the ghosts make a frantic rush for earth to enjoy a month-long holiday — at the expense of human hosts. These are Hungry Ghosts.

Hungry Ghosts are rampaging spirits, restless and homeless. They have been abandoned by unfilial descendants, or are spirits of those who died violent deaths and were never given proper burials. According to a Taoist legend, the gates of hell are opened once a year to allow such spirits to wander among the living.

To placate them, humans make offerings of joss-sticks, food and money at every roadside, cross-roads, temple and other open spaces. These are left at places not too near their homes — for obvious reasons. Few older people like to go out after dark, and only the bold marry during this dangerous month.

At food markets, makeshift tents housing altars are built against a colourful setting of giant joss-sticks. As the festival draws to a close, street theatres or *wayangs* and puppet shows are staged for the, by this time, satiated and satisfied happy ghosts.

The celebration climaxes with a lavish ten-course dinner for man and ghost, followed by an auction of "good-luck" items. Throughout the festival the air is saturated with noise, colour, incense, smoke, lights — all for the Hungry Ghosts.

Nothing is forgotten, especially the disquieting thought that, in a year's time, the happy ghosts will be back again as the Hungry Ghosts!

Mu Lian And The Hungry Ghosts

The Buddhists celebrate the Hungry Ghosts Festival as *Yu Lan Pen* (盂兰盆). "Yu Lan" means "to hang upside down" (in purgatory) and "Pen" is a vessel filled with food offerings. This festival commemorate Mu Lian (目莲) for his filial piety.

According to the legend, Mu Lian's mother, a pious vegetarian, unknowingly drank meat-soup offered by her son and was cured of an acute illness. When Mu Lian told her the truth about the soup, she denied taking the meat, declaring, "If I have eaten meat, let me be cast into the deepest hell!" Immediately she went to hell.

To save his mother, Mu Lian offered to take all the punishment. But as he was placed in a cauldron and about to be sacrificed, Buddha came to his rescue.

After many trials and tribulations Mu Lian located his deceased mother in purgatory among the Hungry Ghosts. When he tried to feed his starving mother, other Hungry Ghosts greedily grabbed the food. On another occasion rice in his mother's mouth turned into fire.

Following Buddha's directions Mu Lian freed his mother from purgatory by offering special prayers and food on the 15th night of the 7th month. Ever since, the Chinese have repeated this practice on behalf of their own ancestors.

One day we ourselves may be with the Hungry Ghosts. Our days are numbered. So let's count each day and let's make each day count, in view of the Chinese saying: "Better be a man for one day than a ghost for a thousand days."

Beware 15th Day!

The Buddhists say: "Those who survive the middle of the 7th month are like iron Buddhas." That's because the dreaded Hungry Ghosts are on the prowl.

To appease these demanding ghosts and send them on their way, food, paper gifts, money and other items are offered and burnt. Besides "Hell Bank" notes, passes designated "Permits for the Souls" are included. A Buddhist service is sometimes held in a marquee for the "King of Devils". Monks, led by the abbot, chant and recite a whole chapter of a sacred book to intercede for the Ghosts' final deliverance from purgatory and enable them to enjoy human food.

At the end of the service, the paper paraphernalia are ignited with some of the food and fruit.

The burning of joss-papers at roadsides and on grass patches has become so widespread, especially on the 15th night, that in Singapore, special containers have to be provided to control environmental pollution and damage. Even then, indiscriminate and inconsiderate burning go on, stirring up ill-feelings between neighbours.

So come the 15th day of this dangerous month, beware Hungry Ghosts and angry ghosts, charred joss-paper and flying ashes, littered earth and polluted air!

To Hell And Back

Taoists believe that after death, one journeys through hell and returns reincarnated to earth in seven week! The tour's itinerary:

1st Week   The traveller reaches the "Demon Gate Barrier". If he has no money to pay the demons he is assailed, beaten and stripped.

2nd Week   He is weighed in the balances. If found to be heavy with sin, he is sawn asunder and ground to powder. (A two-sided fan later restores him to his former condition.)

3rd Week   His next stop is "Bad Dog Village". If he is evil, fierce beasts tear him to pieces until his blood flows in rivers.

4th Week   He peeps into the gigantic "Mirror of Retribution" and sees the doom awaiting him.

5th Week   He is forced to look at the loved ones he has left behind on earth and suffers mental anguish.

6th Week   He reaches the "Bridge of Sighs" spanning the "Inevitable River" that teems with snakes. He is forced to cross this bridge which is 100,000 feet high and 13/10 inches wide!

7th Week He finally heads for the abode of the "King of Wheel". On the way he visits a resthouse where "Madam Meng" (孟婆) offers him a free cup of tea to quench his thirst and wash away all memories of the journey. He is then driven towards the great "Wheel of Law". At the appropriate turn of the wheel of reincarnation he is let loose to return to earth as a human, animal, bird, fish or insect — depending on whether he was good or evil in his previous life.

The Hungry Ghosts, who are considered in limbo (belonging neither to the living nor dead) are barred from this journey to hell and back. Of the living and the dead who are eligible, the Chinese saying makes this confession: "The living man doesn't know his soul; the dead man doesn't know his corpse."

Lucky Humans

"The weariest dragon will mount to heaven sooner or later; why then should not man stumble upon good luck?" goes the encouraging Chinese saying.

One opportunity to stumble upon good luck would be the finale of the Hungry Ghosts Festival, which culminates in a rousing dinner for all believers — who are designated lucky humans. The highlight of the dinner is the auction of a wide range of "lucky items".

After an offering to the Hungry Ghosts comes the distribution of these items. Every diner is entitled to a share, which includes rice, oil, canned food, poles of sugar-cane and assorted fruit packed in a bucket. During dinner, the auction begins. The most sought-after item is the *wu jin* or "black gold" — a piece of charcoal wrapped in gold paper. It comes from an altar of Da Po Gong, God of Prosperity.

Other lucky items include a "prosperity" incense-burner, appliances, a decorated rice barrel and a good-luck tangerine and statues of deities. All these are auctioned off and fetch ten to twenty times their normal prices. The black gold is probably the most expensive item; bids open around $500 and can sometimes rocket up to $100,000 or more!

The lucky bidder and owner displays the black gold on an altar with a god placed upon it, and an incense-burner in front. For a whole year the black gold supposedly protects the owner's wealth and brings him more gold — real gold!

But just in case you feel tempted to go for yellow gold, take a lesson from the Chinese proverb: "There is plenty of yellow gold around, but how many white-haired old friends?"

Happy Ghosts

"**E**very great feast has its last course" — the Chinese saying reminds.

The Hungry Ghosts Festival amounts to a month-long feast during the 7th lunar month. It last course: a street opera to entertain Hungry Ghosts during the finale dinner and "lucky auction". The *ge tai* or "song-stage" shows are those noisy road shows which evolved from the heyday of the Chinese *wayang* or opera in the '50s and '60s. These add colour and noise to the dinner and auction at night. But in the '70s, opera declined and the *ge tai* road shows crept in to attract the younger crowd.

The Chinese believe that, to be happy, the dead should enjoy the same things as the living. But in trying to please both ghosts and humans they get carried away. To attract as many people as possible to watch the shows, it is not uncommon to have sequinned songstresses belt out the latest Chinese and English pop hits on creaky makeshift stages. As requests flow in, the repertoire would include cha-cha-cha, rock-'n'-roll and soul numbers.

To Hungry Ghosts the finale means happiness and satisfaction. To hungry businessmen it means big money and good luck. And it is this last course that brings this fearful festival to a happy conclusion — a resounding success — a Happy Ghost Festival!

Mid-Autumn Festival

Zhong Qiu Jie • *Mooncake Festival*

The traditional Mid-Autumn Festival *Zhong Qiu Jie* (中秋节), celebrated on the 15th day of the 8th lunar month, is better known as the Mooncake or Lantern Festival.

The happy festival may have begun as a harvest thanksgiving celebration, coinciding with the harvest season in China — always an occasion for rejoicing.

The festival was first celebrated by high-ranking officials in northern China during the Sung dynasty. These officials used to exchange gifts of round mirrors to represent and reflect the full moon, and also as "dew-collecting basins".

These symbolic gifts signified complete success in all their undertakings and also good health (by removing the "dew" that causes backaches and rheumatic pains). These dew-collecting basins were also to forestall wet weather during the harvest season. In addition, the people consumed "flirting-with-the-moon broth". But there were no mooncakes or lanterns.

Eventually the common people joined in the celebrations, feasting and rejoicing heartily over their harvests.

The "moon" part of the festival probably originates from an old ceremony paying homage to the moon. In Chinese culture, the moon is spiritually more important than the sun, inspiring even the calendar. Farming is closer in rhythm with the moon than the sun. The phases of the moon even affect the menstrual cycle — and mental cycles too!

No wonder, on this 15th night, when the moon is supposed to be at its fullest and brightest, there are more moonstruck "lunatics" than on any other night!

Moon Worship

As foreign astronauts orbit the moon in outer space, the Chinese worship the moon in open space — outside their houses. In the open air a table is laid out with an incense pot and lighted joss-sticks in it. Behind this pot are placed mooncakes, groundnuts, pomelos, melons, wine and cups of tea.

The ceremony is accompanied by the customary lighting of joss-sticks and red candles and the burning of joss-papers. The joss-paper is of the gold-leaf variety used by gods. (The silver variety is used only for the dead.)

With some families a lighted galloping-horse lantern is a must because moonlight is believed to have the speed of a horse. With other families, boxes of face-powder and cosmetics are also placed on the altar. After prayers these articles are endowed with the power of beautifying the complexion.

At the same time, the moon is invoked to bless the female devotees with handsome, robust and intelligent offspring.

In China an offering of 13 mooncakes of varying sizes are piled up like a pyramid to signify a complete Chinese lunar year plus an intercalary month, making a total of 384 days — a complete cycle of happiness.

Fruits offered in sacrifice have symbolic meanings: hardy and sturdy gourds express the wish for long-lasting family unity; pomegranates, filled with seeds, symbolize many children; apples augur peace because the word for "apple" (*ping*) sounds like the word for peace; and the round mooncake signifies complete family unity.

Despite paying homage to the moon, imperfect man — like a broken drum — may sometimes save the object of his worship, especially during a lunar eclipse. Such an eclipse is dreaded by the Chinese, who believe that a celestial dog has the moon in its jaws and is about to swallow it. Drums are beaten, creating noise to drive away the monster dog.

The Chinese way succeeds every time: the moon always emerges unscathed after every encounter! Now you know why the Chinese proudly proclaim the proverb: "Even a broken drum can save the moon!"

Moon Magic

The magical full moon of the 8th lunar month constitutes the very soul of the Mid-Autumn Festival. Under its spell Chinese lovers are drawn irresistibly together in holy matrimony. The Old Man on the Moon — the divine matchmaker — registers their marriages according to his records.

The moon has become a deeply ingrained symbol of love predestined by the Old Man, the God of Marriage. And what the Old Man has put together, let no man put asunder! Because of its perfectly circular shape, the full moon has also become a symbol of well-rounded family togetherness.

The purity of its silvery rays has so instilled confidence in people that it often provides a celestial witness to their vows.

In Chinese literature Yu Boya, a prominent official, smashed his priceless *qin* (a musical instrument) as a sacrifice to his dead friend Zhong Ziqi, the only person who appreciated his music. A year before they had become sworn brothers before the full moon.

The Mid-Autumn Festival used to inspire "moon appreciation" parties. All that were required were mooncakes and fruits and, of course, lanterns for the children. Admirers picnicked and gazed at the full moon, drinking in its magical light.

The great Tang poet laureate Li Bai — a wine lover — wrote beautiful poetry extolling the moon. He was reputed to have drowned in a lake while trying to embrace the moon's reflection in the water from a boat. Apparently, he was under the influence of drink. More likely, though, it was the magic spell of the mid-autumn full moon!

Mooncakes And Lanterns

Because of its association with mooncakes and lanterns, the Mid-Autumn Festival is today known as the Mooncake or Lantern Festival. The mooncake is shaped like a drum the size of a small saucer, and filled with lotus seed or red bean paste and melon seeds. A salted duck's egg yolk, symbolizing the moon, forms its core. When the cake is sliced in the middle the golden yolk resembles the full moon.

The Mooncake Festival is celebrated by eating mooncakes. Some families bake one large cake and each member eats a piece to foster unity. Children display paper lanterns in the shape of rabbits, fish, birds and butterflies. Nowadays other figures include aeroplanes, rockets, tanks, TV characters and singing idols.

As early as one month before the festival, mooncakes and lanterns are sold. Mooncakes are also offered to ancestors. For good luck, gifts are always offered in pairs, so another gift is added — the pomelo. The pomelo symbolizes prosperity because the Cantonese name for pomelo is *yow* which sounds like "to have".

Besides mooncakes, there are wheat-flour cakes moulded into different shapes — fish, crab, an old man, lion, dragon and also a pig in a bamboo poke.

Mooncakes are specially offered to the moon on the 15th night to promote harmony between man and moon. Despite countless years of such offerings we still have moonstruck lunatics around. What we need desperately are not "mooncakes" but "mancakes" — to promote harmony between man and man!

Mooncake, Mongols And Manchus

Never underate the power of the mooncake. Just as the moon can exert a powerful influence on humans, so can the mooncake.

Mooncakes once played an important part in liberating China from the hated Mongols in the 14th century. The Mongols, to counter subversion, billeted their soldiers in Chinese households. This tightened security led to greater friction with the Chinese, who organized a revolt. Secret messages naming Rebellion Day were hidden in mooncakes and passed from neighbour to neighbour under the very noses of the Mongol soldiers. The revolt against Mongol rule was successful, and in 1368 the first emperor of the Chinese Ming dynasty ascended the Dragon Throne.

According to Chinese sources, mooncakes were first mentioned in connection with the Mid-Autumn Festival only when China came under Manchu rule much later. The oppressive yoke of the Manchu regime led to an exodus of Chinese to various parts of Southeast Asia. The emigrants carried abroad their culture and traditions, including the offering of the mooncake purely in honour of the moon, without any connection with the harvest festival, the Mongols or the Manchus.

So on Mooncake Festival Day: remember the moon; forget the Mongols and the Manchus!

Moon Gods And Goddesses

When westerners claimed that they had landed on the moon, they must have been out of their minds!

The sacred moon is the realm of Chang-E, the moon goddess. She was the beautiful wife of Hou Yi, the archer who saved the world by shooting down nine suns with his arrows.

In those days ten suns circled the earth. One day all ten appeared together, scorching the earth with their heat. The great archer shot down nine of them and was rewarded by the king. Hou Yi turned into a boorish tyrant. To save the people from his oppressive rule, Chang-E stole from him the pill of immortality and swallowed it. She found herself floating to the moon.

The pill made Chang-E ill. She vomited and turned into a white rabbit and then into a three-legged toad.

Thus started the legend of the lady on the moon to whom young Chinese maidens would pray at the Mid-Autumn Festival. Chang-E must have made the first mooncake.

On the moon there is a cinnamon tree in the Moon Palace. It grows so fast that it would overshadow the brilliance of the moon if left untrimmed. So the Woodcutter God Wu Gang is there to check its growth with his axe.

The Old Man on the Moon — the God of Marriage — is there also to arrange marriages because "Marriages are made in heaven but prepared on the moon." And of course, there are the beautiful and graceful moon-fairies.

The "moon" that the foreign astronauts claimed to have landed on has no atmosphere, no woodcutter or old man, no white rabbit or three-legged toad, let alone a moon goddess and beautiful fairies. The poor moonstruck "astro-nuts" must have landed somewhere else!

Double Ninth Festival

Ninth Day Of Ninth Month

The Double Ninth Festival *Chong Yang Jie* (重阳节) is a celebration held on the 9th day of the 9th lunar month. Ancient Chinese cosmology developed along dualistic lines based on the *Yin* and *Yang* principles. Yin is symbolic of the earth, darkness and the female principle. Yang represents the sun, light and the male principle.

All odd numbers are regarded as Yang. So the 9th day of the 9th month is a double Yang day, hence the name *Chong Yang Jie*. (*Chong* means "repeat".) To the Chinese the number nine is highly significant and auspicious.

The Double Ninth Festival in old China was a day for climbing hills to enjoy nature in autumn. It was a day for peaceful relaxation, eating cakes, drinking chrysanthemum wine, and composing or reciting poetry.

The ninth month also heralded the approach of winter. Filial Chinese felt that just as the living needed warm clothing to weather the cold months ahead, their dead ancestors should be provided with warm clothing. The Double Ninth Festival was another occasion, besides Qing Ming Jie, for a visit to the graves of family members. So, to keep their ancestors warm and lively, winter clothes made of paper were despatched to the other world posthaste — through fire! And what a fitting way too, for the Chinese words for "fire" (*huo*) and for "living" (*huo*) are phonetically identical.

To the dead fire means life!

Ascending The Heights

The Chinese proverb asks "Without climbing the mountain, how do you expect to see the plain?"

An opportunity to literally climb the mountain occurs during the Double Ninth Festival. This festival originated with the custom of *deng gao* (登高), ascending the heights. The word *deng* means to "mount". The word *gao*, meaning "height" implies promotion and rhymes with the word for "cake" (糕). So the expression *deng gao* metaphorically refers to a promotion, and eating the cake signifies success.

The word "ninth" is *jiu* (九) which puns with "a long time". (久) From the doubling of "ninth" comes the expression *jiu jiu* (九九) a term homonymous with "a very long time" (久久) — a very long span of life.

In China the autumn sky was usually clear, an ideal time for scaling the heights to picnic and enjoy the panoramic view. High-ranking officials and scholars made it a point on this day to go on excursions, eat festival cakes and drink chrysanthemum wine. Blooming in autumn, the chrysanthemum is associated with the 9th month and symbolizes autumn.

Its name *ju* (菊) is phonetically close to the words for "to remain" (*ju*), "nine" (*jiu*) and "long time." (*jiu*) So the chrysanthemum also symbolizes longevity.

Today the practice of "ascending the heights" is better known as the Double Ninth Festival and emphasizes a "repeat" visit to ancestors' cemeteries with offerings of food and paper clothing. But it's no more an ascent to the heights above; it's a descent to the depths below — to the world of ancestors!

Double Ninth Legends

The origin of "ascending the heights" during the Double Ninth Festival can be traced to a legend concerning an eccentric Taoist prophet, a hermit who lived in the mountains. This prophet Huan Jing advised his friend Fei Chang-fang to flee to the mountain to avoid a calamity. Chang-fang spent the whole day up the hills with his family. When they returned home in the evening Chang-fang found his dogs and poultry had died as their substitutes. This happened on the ninth day of the ninth month.

Another legend concerns a wicked emperor who, fearing that a prophet-exorcist might overthrow him, killed the prophet and his eight brothers, put their heads in a casket and threw it into the sea. A fisherman who found the casket heard a voice inside imploring him to tear off a strip of red paper that sealed the lid. The terrified man obeyed and the nine heads flew to heaven, only to return later to warn him of an impending calamity — a flood. They told him to build a strong raft and to put lamps on it. In the flood the fisherman and his friends were saved and the wicked emperor died.

In both stories the calamity theme exists and the repetition of the number nine, though this does not seem sufficient reason for the Double Ninth Festival to persist. The ordinary Chinese is involved with the pursuit of success, the appeasement of the spirits and the seeking of knowledge of the future. All this is effected by paying ritualistic respect to the spirits by divination and by heeding any prophetic messages, good or bad, if it is to his advantage.

As the Chinese saying puts it: "The false prophet who foretells calamity and the true prophet who predicts health should both be cherished."

Nine-Emperor God

"The prison is always shut and always full; the temple is always open and always empty" — goes the old Chinese saying. For the first nine days of the ninth month, however, the temple is always full.

It becomes the nerve centre of worship and prayer, a scene of hustle and bustle. Inside, devotees mill around, praying with joss-sticks and burning joss-paper. Outside, hawkers ply their wares — flowers, amulets, charms and yellow flags. And if the compound is big enough, a *wayang* goes on at full volume, an opera specially staged for the deities.

Charms are bought for the home and to wear. Another type is to be burnt to ashes, diluted with tea or water and drunk. The object of the people's worship is the Nine-Emperor God — a composite god made up of nine former emperors, best known by the Hokkien collective name *Kau Ong Yah* (九皇爷). The nine emperor gods are mythological figures, sons of the Queen of Heaven. These gods control the fortune, health and longevity of their devotees.

On the ninth day the urn containing sandalwood and the spirit of the Nine-Emperor God is given a ceremonial send-off. It is loaded into a decorated *sampan*, a small boat, and then set adrift, marking the end of the festival. The Chinese then warn: "On the ninth day of the ninth month travellers should steer clear of the lakeside."

The Nine-Emperor God is represented by an idol seated on a lotus pedestal. It has four pairs of hands, two are clasped in meditation and each of the other six holds the sun, the moon, a big seal, a sword, a spiked club and a bow with arrows.

Fear underlies the violent rituals required to placate the gods: firewalking by devotees and mediums who slash their tongues, smear the blood on yellow paper and sell them as charms! These mediums also carry a sedan chair rocking wildly as it bears the Nine-Emperor God across the firepit!

Sounding a note of warning against spirit forces is the Chinese saying: "Three feet above your head the air is thick with spirits!"

DATE DUE